CW00502460

650+ Memory Prompts
for your AutoBiography, Memoir or Life Story

RAYMOND DAVEY

Copyright © 2017 Raymond Davey

All rights reserved.

ISBN: 9781521417324

CONTENTS

About the Author

When my grandfather died in 1980, I was a young lad; and like most young lads at that time I had no real interest or appreciation of my family history. It was not until 35 years later, when I started researching my family tree, that I realized how little I knew about my grandfather's life.

As I had left the UK when I was 5 years old, I had not been around for the last 10 years of my grandfather's life. Sadly, I had not been able to share time with him to listen to his stories, hear him sing (he had an amazing voice), or find out about his dreams and aspirations. While he had earned several medals in WWII, my grandfather's military history has drawn a complete blank. My grandmother would have been the only other person that could have helped fill in the blanks. Unfortunately she is now suffering from late stage dementia and unable to remember anything from the past. Sadly I have left it too late to ask.

After talking to friends, acquaintances and other family members, I found it to be a common theme. We all have grandparents we know very little about, parents who have amazing stories – but nothing is ever recorded, and we all know people who have had life limiting illnesses and were taken before their children had grown into adults. There are so many stories and dreams that are lost. The wisdom and knowledge of older generations are not being passed down around the table or beside the fireplace like they used to be.

I wondered why more people don't write their family histories. It turns out it is not for lack of trying!

Often people don't know what to write about, or have trouble recalling important events – or they simply don't have the time to complete the task.

The Questions

The questions in this book have been carefully selected to provide a plan that will bring out the interesting and detailed accounts of your life. The questions are structured to gather the information that defines you who you are, and the things that are most important to you.

They have been written so they can be used as a guide when you are writing your own autobiography/memoir, or as a comprehensive source of questions to use when interviewing a family member to capture memories before they are gone.

From your childhood memories, through your early schooling and middle years, and up into your senior years, we have made sure that each part of your life is covered. There are hundreds of questions broken into the different stages of life.

To round things out we include sections related to further education, marriage, children, migration, business success and failures and detailed military history questions. Of course, no autobiography would be complete without reflecting on the impact of world landmark events. (eg. The Moon Landing, Assassination of JFK, and 9/11)

Making the most of this list

There are many ways to tackle your autobiography.

A method that seems to work for most people is to print out the pages of this book and sit down with a ball point pen, a highlighter and writing pad.

As you work your way through the main list, use a ball point pen to cross out the questions or sections that don't apply to you (eg some of the military experiences etc)

Once you have done this, select a few questions from each section. Choose memories that are easiest to write about. Use the highlighter to mark the questions that are most interesting and bring back the most memories. You can always come back to the other questions later.

Now, take your writing pad and brainstorm your favourite question from the list. Spend 10 to 15 minutes jotting down a list of things that come to mind. You don't want to fill in the detail at this stage. In most cases, two or three words or a short sentence for each item will be enough to help you revisit the memory when you are writing. As you get used to the process, you will find that the memories come flooding back and you won't be able to write fast enough.

It is important to immediately jot down any memories that come up while you are writing. A short sentence is often best – as single words will quickly lose their context. Always keep a notebook handy or use your mobile phone or tablet to make notes while you are writing.

Now it's time to organize your list into a structure and convert it into a story. You might like to use the internet to lookup events, places, people or objects. Seeing pictures often brings out even more memories. Maybe you have photos in an old album or old family videos.

Remember who your target audience is. If you are writing for your future generations or family, the grammar and spelling doesn't have to be perfect. It is much better to get your story down, than to write a prize winning literary piece.

Finally, remember that writing a life story takes a long time. Some days you may not want to write – and that is OK.

Birth

Topic	Question
Meaning of my Name	Who gave you your name?
Place of Birth	Where were you born?
My Birth	Was your birth natural or were there complications?
Family Traits	Who are you told you looked most like when you were born?
Religion	Were you born into a particular religion?

Childhood – Age 0 to 10

Topic	Question
Local Area	Tell me about the town where you lived as a child.
Childhood Home	What was your childhood home like?
Hideaways	Describe your favourite hiding place or retreat when you were a child
Visiting Old Places	Have you ever gone back to visit the places from your childhood - school, house, playgrounds, parks, etc?
Appearance	Describe your appearance as a child.

Nickname	Did you have a nickname?
Adoption / Foster	If you were raised by anyone other than your parents tell me about this.
Feeling Loved	Did you feel loved as a child?
Earliest Memories	What is your earliest childhood memory?
Friendships	Tell me about friendships you had as a young child and when you were at primary school.
Imaginary Friends	Did you have an imaginary friend at any time?
Typical Day	What was a typical day like when you were a child?
Chores and Pocket Money	Did you have chores as a child?
Music	Tell me about the types of music you heard as a child.
Books / Reading	What kind of reading material would typically be found in your home?
Favourites	Did you have a favourite nursery rhyme, story, television program, movie, song, toy?
Vacations	Did you go on vacation/take day trips as a child?

Family Events	Tell me about a time that you remember your family being together for a special occasion
Stage Shows	Did you ever participate in a school or community performance?
Summer Camp	Did you ever go to camp in the summer?
Birthday Parties	Do you remember having a birthday party as a child?
Special Gifts	Is there a gift you received that stands out in your mind?
Heroes	Did you have heroes as a child?
Beliefs	At what point did you stop believing in Santa Claus, the Tooth Fairy and other childhood fantasies?
Getting Lost	Did you ever get lost as a child?
Accomplishments	Is there something you did as a child that made you feel valued or important?
Encouragement	Were you encouraged as a child?
Rules	What rules did you have to obey as a child in your family?
Restrictions	What were some of the things you wanted to do as a child but could not?
Risky and Dangerous	What type of things did you get up to as a child that felt risky or dangerous?
Jealousy	What things made you jealous as a child?

Health	How was your health as a child?
Religion	Describe your family's spiritual beliefs.
Taboo Topics	What issues were taboo in your household?
Finances	What was your perception of your family's financial circumstances?
Mother	Describe your mother as she was then.
Father	Describe your father as he was then.
Brothers / Sisters	Tell me about each of your brothers/sisters from youngest to oldest.
Grandparents	What do you remember about your grandparents as a child?
Pets	Tell me about any pets you had as a child.
Relationships	What do you remember about your parent's relationship with each other?
Special Talents	Was anyone in your family talented or particularly gifted at something?
Favourite Relative	Apart from your parents did you have a favourite relative?
Pre-School / Day Care	Did you attend pre-school or day-care as a child?

First Days at School	Do you remember your first day at school?
Excitement	Do you remember shopping for school clothes and stationery?
School Memories	What types of school(s) did you attend?
School Lunches	What was your lunch routine at school?
Teachers	Do any of your teachers stand out in your mind?
Crushes	Did you ever have a crush on any of your teachers or schoolmates?
Report Cards	What were your report cards like?
Favourite Subjects	What were your favourite subjects at school?
Physical Education	Did you like physical education / gym class?
Classmates	What do you remember about your classmates?
Getting to School	How did you travel to and from school?
Getting into Trouble	Do you remember getting into trouble at school?
Field Trips	Do you remember any field trips your class took?
School	What did you do when there was no school?

Holidays	
Music	Did you ever play a musical instrument or take part in the school choir, stage shows etc?
In Front of the Class	Do you remember having to stand up in front of the class to read a paper or a story?
Reading and Writing	Did you write your b, d and p, q back to front?
Clique	Were you in a clique at school?
Useful Life Lessons	What did you learn in school that you still use to this day?
Regrets	What do you wish you would have learned more about in school?
Outside School	Tell me about activities that you took part in outside school.
Fears	What were your childhood fears?
Death	Did anyone close to you die at this time?
Difficult Times	Do you remember any difficult times throughout your childhood?
Summing Up	How would you sum up your childhood years
Wisdom	If you were given the opportunity to sit down with yourself as a child what advice would you give based on your experiences?

Teenage Years – Age 11 to 17

Topic	Question
Local Area	Describe the town(s) you lived in.
Teenage Home	Tell me about your home(s) during these years.
Appearance	What did you wear through your teenage years?
Pets	Tell me about any pets you had as a teenager.
Books	What books did you read as a teenager?
Music	What type of music did you like to listen to during these years?
Dancing	Did you enjoy dancing?
Leisure Time	Describe what you did in your leisure time for enjoyment.
Friday/Saturday Nights	Describe a typical Friday/Saturday night when you were a teenager.
Musical Instruments	Did you learn to play a musical instrument?
Vacations	Did you take any trips/vacations as a family during your teenage years?

Alone Time	During your teenage years did you ever take a trip/vacation alone?
Learning to Drive	Do you remember when you learned to drive?
First Car/Bike	Do you remember your first vehicle?
Working	Did you work during your teenage years?
Health	How was your health during your adolescence?
Birthdays	Can you recall a birthday from your teenage years?
Coming of Age	How did your family mark your coming of age?
Special Occasions	Tell me about a time when your family came together for a special occasion.
Travel	How did you get around when you were a teenager?
News	How did you learn what was happening in the world around you?
Finances	What were the financial circumstances of your family at this time (poor, average, rich)?
Cost of Living	Where did you buy food, clothing, furniture, etc?
Difficulties	Can you remember any particular times of sadness, doubt, anxiety, embarrassment, etc?

Confidence Building	Did you ever do something as a teenager that you still can't believe you did?
High School	Tell me about your High School(s) during your teenage years.
First Day at High School	Do you remember your first day at high school?
Typical Day	Tell me about a typical school day.
Lunch Routine	What was your lunch routine at high school?
Most Memorable Year	Choose a memorable year at high school.
Choices	What was the attitude of your parents to your schooling and the choices that lay ahead of you?
Goals	What goals did you have for yourself?
Outside School	Aside from your normal classes what other activities were you involved in at school?
Leaving School	When did you leave high school?
Regrets	Looking back on your teenage years at school are there subjects or interests you wish you had taken further?
Social Events	What social gatherings and events did you attend through high school

Behaviours	What was acceptable behaviour concerning dating, sex, alcohol, drugs, smoking, etc, when you were a teenager?
Getting in Trouble	Did you ever get into trouble as a teenager?
Relationships	How did you get along with your family at this time
Out of Touch	Did you feel 'out of touch' with your parents at this time?
Disagreements	Do you remember any friction or disagreements within your family at this time?
Being Embarrassed	Did your parents ever embarrass you?
Friendships	Who were your friends during these years?
First Date	Describe your first date.
Boyfriend/Girlfriend	Did you have many boyfriends/girlfriends during your teenage years?
Romance	Did any of your dates turn into a romantic relationship?
Crushes	Did you ever develop a crush on anyone at this time?
Reputation	Were you aware of what others thought of you?
True Love	Did you meet a 'true love' at this time in your life?

Sex Education	Do you recall how you learned about the facts of life?
Transitions	Can you recall the transition from child to young adult?
Feelings	How would you describe this time in your life?
Acceptance	Where did you feel most accepted during these teenage years?
Confidence	Were you particularly self-conscious at this time?
Dreams	What was important to you during these years?
Lessons Learnt	When you think of your teenage years now how would you describe yourself then?
Spiritual	What were your spiritual beliefs at this time?
Really Bad Things	Did anything particularly bad happen to you
Death	Did anyone close to you die at this time?
Memories	When you think back on your teenage years now, which memories do you most and least enjoy?
Wisdom	If you were given the opportunity to sit down with yourself as a teenager what advice would you give based on your experiences?
Appearance	Describe your physical appearance at this time.

Early Adult – Age 18 to 24

Topic	Question
Early Adulthood Home	Tell me about your home(s) during these years.
Relationships	Describe what was happening in your family at this time.
Leaving Home	If you left the family home during these years describe the day you left.
Occupation	What was your occupation job during these years?
College/University	If you didn't go to college/university do you think you were at a disadvantage?
Changes	Describe some of the changes you faced at work during these years.
Out of Work	Were you ever forced to leave a job through redundancy, site closure, being fired, etc?
Homemaker	If you were a homemaker at this time describe what you did.
Favourite Stories	What were your favourite stories or memories from your early days at work?
Least Favourite Stories	What were your least favourite stories or memories from your early days at work?
Finances	Describe your financial circumstances.

Birthdays	Do you recall a birthday from early adulthood?
Special Occasions	Describe a time your family came together for a special occasion during these years.
Pets	Did you have a pet during these years?
Clubs and Sport	Were you involved in any clubs, sports, groups or organizations at this time?
Hobbies	Tell me about any hobbies/passions you had at this time.
Travel/Vacations	Did you go on any vacations/trips/outings?
Vehicles	Do you remember your vehicles during this time?
Friendships	Who were your friends at this time?
Pressures	Within your circle of friends what pressures did you face?
Risks	What type of things did you do at these times that were risky, adventurous or thrilling?
Firsts	Remember some firsts during this time
Dating	Did you do much dating during these years?
The Dating Game	Reflect back on your relationships at this time in your life.
True Love	Did you meet a 'true love' at this time in your life?

Health	How was your health at this time?
Choices	When you think back to this time in your life how would you describe yourself?
Growing Up	Did you feel more like an adult as you left your teens and moved into your twenties?
Difficulties	Tell me about some of your more difficult times during these years.
Fears / Worries	What were your fears and worries during this period of your life?
Inspiration	Can you think of someone at this time that influenced and inspired you?
Spiritual	What were your spiritual beliefs at this time?
Politics	What age were you when you were able to vote?
Values	At what point do you think you developed your own set of values and beliefs?
Hopes and Dreams	What hopes and dreams did you have for your future?
Memories	When you think back to your early adult years now, which memories do you most and least enjoy?
Wisdom	If you were given the opportunity to sit down with yourself as a young adult what advice would you give based on your

	experiences?

Further Education

Topic	Question
Location	Where was your college/university located?
Living Arrangements	Where did you live during your college/university years?
Strengths and Weaknesses	At college/university what would you say were your strengths and weaknesses?
Lecturers / Teachers	Do you remember any of your teachers/lecturers?
Work	Did you work to support yourself while you studied?
Social Events	What social gatherings and events did you attend through college/university
Graduation	At the end of your studies did you graduate?

Adulthood – Age 25 to 44

Topic	Question
Appearance	Describe yourself at this time.
Towns / Cities	Tell me about the town(s) you lived in

	during these years.
Home	Tell me about your home(s) during these years.
Parents	Describe your mother and father as they were at this time.
Relationships	How was your relationship with your parents at this time?
Family Get Together	Describe a time when your family came together during these years.
Occupation	How were you earning a living during this time?
Promotion	Which stages in your career and personal life were significant during these years?
Finances	What were your financial circumstances during these years?
Homemaker	If you were a homemaker describe your work, duties and responsibilities.
Education	Were you studying at this time
Social Life	Did you have an active social life?
Friendships	Who were your friends at this time in your life?
Hobbys	Tell me about a hobby/passion you had during this time.
Travel / Vacations	Tell me about vacations and trips that you

	took at this time.
Getting About	How did you get around at this time
Music	What types of music were you listening to at this time?
Books	What were you reading during these years?
Birthdays	Do you remember a particular birthday(s) from this time (30th, 40th)?
Reunions	Did you go to any reunions during these years
Status	What was your status at this time
True Love	Did you meet a 'true love' at this time in your life?
Health	How was your health at this time?
Politics	What were your political beliefs at this time?
Spiritual	Tell me about your spiritual beliefs at this time.
Death	Did you lose anyone close to you at this time?
Difficulties	What difficult times do you recall from these years?
Dreams	What were your plans, hopes and dreams for the future?

Memories	When you think back on your prime adult years now, which memories do you most and least enjoy?
Regrets	What would you change about your life at this time if you could?
Wisdom	If you were given the opportunity to sit down with yourself during these years what advice would you give based on your experiences?
Significant Events	Were there any significant historical/social events taking place at this time?

Adulthood – Age 45 to 64

Topic	Question
Appearance	Describe your appearance at this time

Town / Cities	Tell me about the town(s) you lived in.
Home	Tell me about your home(s) during these years.
Parents	What do you remember about your mother and father from this time?
Family Events	How did you normally celebrate the big holidays (Christmas, Thanksgiving) during these years?
Occupation	How were you earning a living during this time?
Finances	Describe your financial circumstances at this time.
Homemaker	If you were a homemaker during these years, what did your work entail?
Education	Were you taking any courses/classes at this time in order to improve yourself?
Friendships	Tell me about your friends at this time
Relationships	Who were the main people in your life at this time
Travel / Vacations	What vacations/trips/travels did you have during this time?
Clubs	How did you like to spend your spare time
Relaxation Time	What did you do to relax and unwind after a hard day
Music	What music did you enjoy?
Books	What were you reading at this time?
Birthdays	Describe a memorable birthday from this time (50th,

	60th).
Health	How was your health during these years?
Health Secrets	If you have kept well what is the secret to your good health?
Disputes	During these years did you ever have a bad argument with someone or a falling out?
Plans	What were your plans for retirement?
Provisions	What provisions did you make for retirement
Best of Times	Tell me about some of the best times during this period.
Priorities	What did you feel were your priorities at this time?
Milestones	What were the major milestones in your career and personal life during these years?
Influences	When you think back to your middle years who or what had the greatest influence over you?
Turning Points	Describe some turning points for you at this stage of your life.
Parents	At this stage in your life what was your opinion of the job that your parents did raising you?
Changes	Looking back what would you change about your life at this time and the choices you made?
Political	Describe your political beliefs at this time.
Spiritual	What place did religion have in your life at this time?

Death	Did anyone close to you die at this time?
Difficulties	What were the difficulties you faced at this time?
Memories	When you think back to your middle adult years now, which memories do you most and least enjoy?
Wisdom	If you were given the opportunity to sit down with yourself during these years what advice would you give based on your experiences?
Achievements	What are you most proud of from this time in your life?
Regrets	Did you ever behave in a way you were ashamed of during these years?
Putting Things Off	During these middle years what are some of the things you put off until later?
Advances in Technology	Describe some technological advances and changes you witnessed at this time in your life.
Significant Events	Were there any significant historical/social events taking place during this time?

Older Adult Years – Age 65+

Topic	Question
Appearance	Describe your appearance at this time
Town / City	Tell me about the town(s) you have lived in during your older adult years
Home	Tell me about your home(s) during these years and today.
Best Home	Of all the homes you have lived in over the years which one has meant the most to you?
No Longer Here	Tell me about a place you know that is no longer there as a result of development or destruction.
Friendship	Who have been your friends during these later years?
Family Get Together	Which members of your family do you see and what do you do together?
Holidays	How do you spend the holidays?
Filling the Day	How do you occupy your time these days
Work	If you are still working what is your job?
Retirement	If you retired during this time describe the experience.
Finances	How are you managing financially?

My Life is Blessed	In what ways have you been blessed?
Politics	Describe your social and political beliefs today.
Books	What are you reading at this time
Music	What music are you listening to?
Travel	What trips have you taken recently or in the last few years?
Birthdays / Anniversaries	Describe a memorable birthday or anniversary you have had lately.
My Treasures	What have you saved through the years
Activities I Want To Do	What activities have you thought about trying lately?
Technology	How does technology affect your life today?
Turning Points	Describe some turning points for you at this stage of life.
Life in General	How do you feel about your life today?
Moments in Time	What moments in your life today do you cherish?

Act of Kindness	Tell me about a time when someone's kindness made a real difference to your life.
Romantic Gestures	Tell me about some romantic times and gestures you have experienced.
Prejudice	Were you ever prejudiced, racist or biased towards anyone through the years?
Angry Moments	Tell me about some things that make you mad, angry or sad these days.
Security and Fears	When do you feel most content these days?
Parents	When you think back on your life do you think that your parents would have been proud of you and your accomplishments?
To My Parents and Siblings	How would you say you are like each of your parents and siblings?
Deepest feelings	What memories trigger the deepest feelings in you
Memories	How would you sum up this time in your life?
I've Made a Difference	In what way do you think you make a difference to the lives of those around you
How I Have Changed	Reflect on the years gone by and the person you have become.
Inspiration	Who do you admire today
Wisdom	What is your attitude to life?
Advice for the	What advice would you give to the younger

Younger Generations	generation about life and events?
The Future	What do you find exciting about the future?
Older Age	How do you feel about old age?
Death	Do you ever think about death and dying?
If Only	If you could choose one person to see again who would it be and why?
Spiritual	What are your spiritual beliefs today?
Big Issues	What are your thoughts on topics such as abortion, AIDS, divorce, homosexuality and discrimination?
Stories of My Life	What are the stories of your life that have never before been shared?
Significant Events	What significant historical/social events have you witnessed lately

Military - General History

A note about the military questions: Some of the military questions refer to specific campaigns experienced by ANZAC soldiers from New Zealand and Australia in WWII. While some of the questions may not apply to your specific military experiences, you can often apply the same questions to other theatres of war. We have included additional sections for Navy, Army, Civilian Life, Vietnam, Korea and Iraq/Afghanistan.

Topic	Question
Entering The Military	What age were you when you entered the Military?
Family Feelings	How did your family feel about you entering the Military?
Military Service	How long did you serve in the Military?
Friendships	Talk about your fellow servicemen and in particular any friendships.
Opportunities	What opportunities did you have while in the Military
Favourite Stories	What are your favourite stories from your time in the Military?
Least Favourite Stories	What are your least favourite stories from your time in the Military?
Lessons Learnt	What did you learn from your time in the services?

Military - WWII Greece

Topic	Question
Before Departure	What unit were you assigned to?
Transit and Arrival	How did you get to Greece?
Posting	Where were you posted?
Battle	What was it like being in battle for the first time?
Greece	The defence of Greece has been described as a series of rear-guard actions. What are your thoughts on this?
Equipment	Where did your unit abandon its equipment when it left Greece?
Anzac Day	Was Anzac Day observed in Greece?
Evacuation	Describe your evacuation from Greece.

Military - WWII Crete

Topic	Question
Physical Shape	What was your physical shape at that time?
Expectations	What were your expectations regarding Crete?
Marching	Describe discipline on the march from Chania/Heraklion to camp.
Camp	Where did you camp?

Preparations	What preparations for battle did you make?
The Local Force	Did you have any contact with Cretans before 20 May?
Communications	What was the state of communications (before 20 May and after) Between HQ and your battalion?
Terrain	What was the countryside like?
Weapons	What weapons did you have with you when you arrived in Crete?
Early Air Attacks	What was your reaction to air attacks before 20 May?
German Airborne Invasion	On May 20, when the paratroopers started to arrive, where were you?
Casualties	Someone wrote that the fighting on Crete consisted of 'a lot of bayonet work'. What are your thoughts on this?
The next few days	Describe your experiences over the next few days.
Maleme	Were you involved in counter-attack at Maleme?
Other combat on Crete	Were you involved in other combat on Crete?
Food and Water	How did you get food during the battle?
Commanders	What is your evaluation of military leadership generally and of your immediate

	commanders in the field?
Wounded and Dead	Were you wounded?
Retreat to Sfakia	Describe your experiences on the retreat over the mountains to Sfakia.
The Evacuation	Describe the process of your evacuation.
Alexandria	Describe your journey there (what ship, food on ship, crowding, bombing by Luftwaffe).

Military - WWII North Africa

Topic	Question
Before Departure	What unit were you assigned to?
Transit and Arrival	How did you get to Egypt?
Camp Life	What were the living conditions like in Maadi camp (food, accommodation, alcohol, leave activities and sport).
Desert Life	What are your strongest memories of life in the desert?
Health Issues	Did you ever get an upset stomach?
Air Attacks	How often did you experience enemy air attacks?
Weapons	What weapons did you have?
Terrain	What was the terrain like that you were

	fighting in?
Waiting	What was it like waiting for a battle to begin?
Under Fire	What can you remember of being under fire?
Enemy Forces	What were some of the main enemy battle tactics used against your position?
Bravest Action	Describe the bravest action (friend or enemy) that you witnessed while serving in the war
Near Misses	Did you have any close calls/near misses?
Killing	What were your feelings about killing?
Sleep	Did you ever suffer from lack of sleep?
Battles	Were there any battles that you particularly remember?
Prisoners	Did you ever take prisoners?
Wounded and Dead	Were you wounded?
Messages from Home	How often did you receive mail?
Local language	What slang terms can you remember?
Camp Life	What was the importance of drinking tea?
Cairo	Did you get leave in Cairo?
Soldiers Clubs	Which of the soldiers clubs did you visit?

Cinemas	Did you ever visit the cinemas: Metro, Diana Palace?
Locals	Did you have any contact with Arabs/Egyptians?
Red Light District	Did you ever visit the red-light areas in Cairo?

Military - WWII Italy

Topic	Question
Before departure	What unit were you assigned to?
Transit and Arrival	How did you get to Italy?
Italy compared to North Africa	(If you fought in North Africa earlier) What was your reaction to the new conditions of Italy in winter compared with North Africa?
Living Conditions	What were the living conditions like in the first months in Italy (food, accommodation, alcohol, leave activities and sport).
Terrain	What was the countryside like (mountainous, river plains)?
Communications	What was the state of communications Between HQ and your battalion?
Commanders	What is your evaluation of military leadership generally and of your immediate commanders in the field?
Weapons	What weapons did you have?
Air Attacks	How often did you experience enemy air attacks?
Mines and Booby Traps	What was your attitude towards mines?
Sleep	Did you ever suffer from lack of sleep?
Battle	What can you remember of being under

	fire?
Fear	Which enemy units were feared the most?
Enemy Forces	What were some of the main enemy battle tactics used against your position?
Bravest Action	Describe the bravest action (friendly or enemy) that you witnessed while serving in the war
The Journey	Describe your journey through Italy.
Prisoners	Did you ever take prisoners?
Killing	What were your feelings about killing?
Wounded	Were you wounded?
Civilians	Did you see dead civilians?
Desertion	Were you aware of any cases of desertion?
Message from Home	How often did you receive mail?
Language	What slang terms can you remember?
Out of Battle	What was the importance of drinking tea?
Local Life	How much contact did you have with local people?
Brothels	How many men visited prostitutes?
On Leave	What did you do on leave?

Military - Civilian

Topic	Question
War Declared	Where were you when you heard war had broken out?
Living Conditions	If you were in WWII, what were your living conditions and experiences during the war?
Work	Where did you work before war broke out?
Family	Did your spouse or a family member serve in the conflict?
Travel	Did you travel at all during the war?
Discrimination	Were you or others in your community treated differently because of your gender/ethnicity/race or other factors?
Marriage	Did you or others get married during wartime?
Fear	Did you worry that your side might not win the war, or that the war wouldn't end?
Lasting Effects	What effect did the war have on your physical and mental health or for others you knew?
Recycling	If you were in WWII, did you have to recycle rubber, grease, metals and other commodities?
Civilian Activist	Were you active in peace, political or anti-war activities?

Prisoner of War

Topic	Question
Being Taken Prisoner	How did it happen?
Wounded	Were you wounded?
Interrogation	If you were an officer, were you interrogated?
Sending News Home	When and how did your family hear that you had been taken prisoner?
Transit Camp	Where were you?
POW Camp Arrival	How did you get to the POW camp(s)?
Camp Life	Who commanded the camp?
Work Camps	Did you have any experience of work camps?
Food	What food were you given?
Health	Did you suffer from any illness or disease?
Cigarettes	Did you smoke cigarettes?
Messages from Home	Did you get mail?
Recreation	What sort of recreational things happened in your camp (housie, card games, gambling, sports, plays, musicals, orchestras, lectures, quizzes, crafts)?
Guards	What were your relations with guards like (nicknames, rackets, bribing guards,

	swapping cigarettes for food, etc.)
Other POW's	Were there any particular characters among the other POWs?
Violence	Did you ever witness violence either from guards or among prisoners?
Other Nationalities	What other nationalities were there in the camp?
Religion	What was the role of religion in camp life?
Resistance	Were you ever involved in any secret committees in camps or in resistance activities?
Escape	How often did you talk about the possibility of escaping?
Outside World	How much knowledge did you have of the war?

Liberation	Where were you when you heard that the war had ended?
Europe : The Long March	Where were you at the time you left?
Repatriation	When did you get back home?

Military - Navy

Topic	Question
Decisions	Why did you choose to serve with the navy?
Training	What training did you do at home?
Ships	What sort of ship were you on?
Living Conditions	What were the living conditions like?
Commission	Did you gain a commission, describe this.
Theatres	What theatres did you serve in?
Under Attack	What were your feelings when you were in the war zone or attacked the first time?
Sinking	If the ship was sunk, describe the sinking.
Wounded and Dead	What sort of supplies were there for wounded?
Enemy Contact	Did you have any contact with the enemy (U-boats often approached survivors in

	lifeboats, took captains POW, sometimes gave water and food)?
Operations	Describe how ships were blacked out at night and how there was radio silence, communication by flags and lights, etc.
Port Visits	Which ports did you spend most time in?
Messages from home	Did you get mail when you arrived in port?
Start of D-Day	Were you involved on D-Day?
On Station on D-Day	What happened when you reached your position?

Military - Air Force

Topic	Question
Decisions	Why did you choose to serve with the air force?
Training	Where did you train?
Overseas Training	If you were trained overseas, do you have lasting memories of the place you were trained?
Squadrons and Ranks	Which squadrons were you assigned to?

Aircraft	What sort of planes did you fly in, operationally?
Enjoyment	Did you enjoy flying?
Station	Where were you based?
First Operational Flight	What do you remember of your first operational flight?
Stress and Fear	How did you deal with Fear?
Superstition	Did you have any superstitions about flying?
Your crew	If you were flying with a crew were you close-knit?
Commissioned	Were you commissioned?
Memorable Missions	Describe any particularly memorable operations.
D-Day	Did you fly during D-Day?
Leave	What did you do on leave?
Capture	Were you ever captured?

Military - Korea

Topic	Question
Before Departure	Did you enlist or were you drafted?
Transit and Arrival	How did you get to Korea?
Local people	Upon arriving, what did you think of the indigenous population?

Language	How did you communicate with locals?
Living Conditions	What were the living conditions like in Korea (food, accommodation, alcohol, leave activities and sport).
Terrain	What was the terrain like that you were fighting in?
Weapons	What weapons did you have?
Under Fire	What can you remember of being under fire?
Battle Tactics	What were standard battle tactics employed by your unit and do you think they were effective?
Mines and Booby Traps	What was your attitude towards mines?
Bravest Action	Describe the bravest action (friend or enemy) that you witnessed while serving in the war
Combat	Were there any battles that you particularly remember?
Sleep	Did you ever suffer from lack of sleep?
Killing	What were your feelings about killing?

Communications	What was the state of communications Between HQ and your battalion?
Commanders	What is your evaluation of military leadership generally and of your immediate commanders in the field?
Enemy Forces	What were some of the main enemy battle tactics used against your position?
Prisoners	Did you ever take prisoners?
Wounded and Dead	Were you wounded?
Message from Home	How often did you receive mail?

Military - Vietnam

Topic	Question
Before Departure	Did you enlist or were you drafted?
Transit and Arrival	How did you get to Vietnam?
Local people	Upon arriving, what did you think of the indigenous population?
Language	How did you communicate with locals?

Living Conditions	What were the living conditions like in Vietnam (food, accommodation, alcohol, leave activities and sport).
Terrain	What was the terrain like that you were fighting in?
Weapons	What weapons did you have?
Under Fire	What can you remember of being under fire?
Battle Tactics	What were standard battle tactics employed by your unit and do you think they were effective?
Mines and Booby Traps	What was your attitude towards mines?
Combat	Were there any battles that you particularly remember?
Bravest Action	Describe the bravest action (friend or enemy) that you witnessed while serving in the war
Sleep	Did you ever suffer from lack of sleep?
Killing	What were your feelings about killing?
Communications	What was the state of communications Between HQ and your battalion?
Commanders	What is your evaluation of military leadership generally and of your immediate commanders in the field?

Enemy Forces	What were some of the main enemy battle tactics used against your position?
Prisoners	Did you ever take prisoners?
Wounded and Dead	Were you wounded?
Message from Home	How often did you receive mail?
Brothels	How many men visited prostitutes?

Military - Iraq / Afghanistan

Topic	Question
Before Departure	What unit were you assigned to?
Transit and Arrival	How did you get to Iraq or Afghanistan?
Local people	Upon arriving, what did you think of the indigenous population?
Living Conditions	What were the living conditions like (food, accommodation, alcohol, leave activities and sport).
Terrain	What was the terrain like that you were fighting in?
Weapons	What weapons did you have?
Under Fire	What can you remember of being under

	fire?
Battle Tactics	What were standard battle tactics employed by your unit and do you think they were effective?
Mines, Suicide Bombers and Booby Traps	What was your attitude towards mines, suicide bombers and booby traps?
Bravest Action	Describe the bravest action (friendly or enemy) that you witnessed while serving in the war
Combat	Were there any battles that you particularly remember?
Sleep	Did you ever suffer from lack of sleep?
Killing	What were your feelings about killing?
Communications	What was the state of communications Between HQ and your battalion?
Commanders	What is your evaluation of military leadership generally and of your immediate commanders in the field?
Enemy Forces	What were some of the main enemy battle tactics used against your position?
Prisoners	Did you ever take prisoners?
Wounded and Dead	Were you wounded?
Message from Home	How often did you receive mail?

End of WWII

Topic	Question
End of the War	Do remember the day war ended?
Returning Home	How long after the war did you or your family members return home?
Leaving the Service	Did you want to leave the service?
Getting Back To Normal	What did you do in the months after the war?
Attitudes	If you were in combat, did you feel like you had anything in common with people who had stayed home?
Long Term	As you look back, describe how the war affected the rest of your life.
POW	If you were a POW, do you have any feelings of resentment/dislike/hatred of former captors?
Visiting Again	Have you ever returned to the places you visited or fought at during the war?

Landmark Events

Topic	Question
Sputnik	How did you hear about the news? Do you remember where you were and what you were doing at the time?
First Man In Space	Do you remember where you were and what you were doing at the time?
Cold War and Cuban Missile Crisis	Do you remember where you were and what you were doing at the time?
JFK Assassinated	Do you remember where you were and what you were doing at the time?
Beatlemania	What are your memories from the time?
Vietnam War Protests	What did you think of the Vietnam War?
Moon Landing	Do you remember where you were and what you were doing at the time?
Nixon Resigns	Do you remember the day President Nixon resigned?
Rocky Horror Picture Show	Did you remember the Rocky Horror Picture Show?
Elvis Presley Died	Do you remember the day Elvis Presley died?
Star Wars Movie	Do you remember seeing the first Star Wars movie in 1978?

First Arcade Machines	Do you remember the first game of Pong you saw?
Mt Erebus Crash	How did you hear about the news? Do you remember where you were and what you were doing at the time?
Energy Crisis	Do you remember the oil shock of 1979.
Cellphone	When was the first time you had a cellphone?
Recession	Do you remember the 1980s recession?
Home Computers and Game Consoles	Did you or your family have a home computer?
Launch of the First Space Shuttle	Do you remember where you were and what you were doing at the time?
First Time you heard a CD	Do you remember the first time you heard a music CD or watched your first DVD?
Queens Street Riots (New Zealand)	Were you at or near the riots when they broke out?
Nuclear Tensions of the 1980s	Do you remember the nuclear tensions of the 1980s?
Chernobyl Nuclear Disaster	How did you hear about the news?
Start of the Gulf War	Do you remember where you were and what you were doing at the time?

Princess Diana Death	Do you remember the day Princess Dianna died?
World Trade Center - 9/11	Do you remember where you were and what you were doing at the time?
Indian Ocean Tsunami	How did you hear about the news?
Hurricane Katrina	How did you hear about the news?
Global Financial Crisis of 2008	Did you get caught up in the global financial crisis?
Japan Tsunami	How did you hear about the news?

Migration

Topic	Question
Home Country	What country were you originally from?
Reasons	Why did you leave your home country?
Making the Move	When did you leave?
Arriving	Can you remember your arrival?
Reflection	What were your hopes for yourself (and/or your family) when you came here?

Business

Topic	Question
Type of Business	What type of business did you run?
Business Partners	Were you in business with anyone else?
Role Models	Did you have any business role models or influencers that you followed in the footsteps of?
Highlights	If your business was successful, what would you attribute it to?
Difficult Times	Did you have any difficult times?
Family Life	How did running a business affect your family life?
Lessons	If your business failed, did owning a business teach you any lessons in life?
Stories	Do you have any great stories or memories from running your business?
Selling the Business	Did you manage to sell the business?

Marriage

Topic	Question
How We Met	How did you meet your spouse?
Courtship	Tell me about your courtship.

The Proposal	Describe the proposal.
The Engagement	How did you celebrate your engagement?
Memories	What do you remember about your spouse from those days
Meeting The Family	Do you remember meeting each other's families for the first time?
Friends	What did you think of each other's friends?
Preparing for the Wedding	In the run up to your wedding what do you remember?
The Night Before the Wedding	Did you have an evening with friends before your wedding day to celebrate your last days of being single?
The Big Day	What can you remember about your wedding day?
The Reception	Was there a celebration after the ceremony?
The Honeymoon	Did you go on a honeymoon?
The First Year	What was your first year of marriage like?
Daily Routines	What was your daily routine in the first year of marriage
Highs and Lows	In those early years what were some of the highs and lows in your marriage?
Establishing Roles	How were your roles defined?

Special Qualities	What was special about your spouse?
Worst Times	What are the worst times you can remember during your marriage?
Best Times	What are the best times you can remember during your marriage?
Outside Influences	What other forces had an effect on your marriage
Regrets	Looking back over your years together what regrets do you have?
Making it Work	What made your marriage work?
Having Children	If you had children how did their arrival affect your relationship?
Not Having Children	If you didn't have children together, why did you not?
The Ex	Were either of you involved with someone else when you met?
Comparing It To My Parents	When you think of your parent's marriage are there any similarities between theirs and yours?

Being Apart	Were you ever apart for any length of time?
Friends and Other Couples	As a couple which friends did you see regularly?
Individualities	Did you have individual interests separate from your spouse?
Special Gifts	What memorable gifts did you give to your spouse or receive from him/her through the years?

Divorce

Topic	Question
Why It Happened	If you have divorced what were the events that led to this?
Support	What support did you get from your family and friends at this difficult time?
Feelings About Divorce	What was your attitude to divorce before this happened to you?
How It Affected the Children	If you had children how did your divorce affect them?
Coping	How did you cope after the divorce?
Relationships with the Ex	How was your relationship with your ex-spouse after the divorce
Looking Back	Looking back is there anything you could have done to save your marriage?

Widowed

Topic	Question
Coping	If you have been widowed how did you cope with losing your partner?
Ceremony	Was there a ceremony to mark his/her passing?
Feelings	In the weeks following your loss how did you feel
Reflection	What would you change about your choices at the time?
Family and Friends	How did your relationship with family and friends change after the death of your spouse?
Source of Strength	Who was your greatest source of strength following your partner's death?
Pushing the Boundaries	Were there things you had to do but didn't feel able or ready for?
Loneliness	Describe your loneliness in the time since your partner died.
Finances	What were your financial circumstances in the time after your partner's death?
Possessions	Of your partner's things what did you keep?
Memories	How do you, your family and friends remember your partner?

Getting Back On Track	Since your partner passed away what have you done to get your life back on track?

Loss of a Parent

Topic	Question
Memories	What things did you keep?
Coping	If you have been lost a parent, how did you cope?
Ceremony	Was there a ceremony to mark his/her passing?
Feelings	In the weeks following your loss how did you feel
Reflection	What would you change about your choices at the time?
Source of Strength	Who was your greatest source of strength following the death?
Pushing the Boundaries	Were there things you had to do but didn't feel able or ready for?

Sadness	Describe your grief in the time since your loss.

Your Children - When They Were Young

Topic	Question
Finding Out	What were your thoughts when you found out you were expecting your first child?
The Birth	Describe the births of your children.
Adoption / Foster	If you adopted a child or children tell me about the day you brought them home.
The First Moments	Tell me about the first moments with your new child.
How It Felt	How did you feel as a first time parent?
Family and Friends React	What was the reaction of your family and friends to your new child/children?
Education	Where did you gain your knowledge about children and parenting?
Daily Routines	Where did you live when your children were young?
Being Apart	Under what circumstances would you be apart from your child/children?

What They Were Like	Describe your children at every age and stage
Activities	What activities did you enjoy doing the most with your children as babies, toddlers, etc?
Starting School	Do you remember when your children started school?
School Days	Tell me about the schools your children attended.
Friends	Do you remember the friends your children had at different ages?
Travel / Vacations	Tell me about a memorable family vacation.
Christmas and Birthdays	How did you celebrate Christmas, Thanksgiving, Birthdays, etc with your children when they were young?
Eating Habits	Describe each of your children's eating habits.
Chores	Did you give your children chores?
Discipline	Describe your philosophy for bringing up children.
Interests	What were your children's interests?
Pets	What pets did your children have through the years?
Proud Parent	What makes you proud when you think of your child/children?
Worries and Fears	What were your main worries and fears as a parent?
Tastes and	As your children grew up and developed their own

Influences	tastes what did you observe about each of them?
Health	How was your children's health?
Other Role Models	Apart from you and your partner which other adults played an important role in your child's life?
Encouragement	How did you encourage your child?
Firsts	What firsts do you remember for each child

Your Children - Older Years

Topic	**Question**
Teenage Difficulties	What difficulties did your child have as a teenager?
Traumatic Experience	Did any of your children ever go through a traumatic experience?
Changing Relationship	As your children grew into adults how did your relationship with them change?
Older Lives	What lives did your children make for themselves

Your Children - Reflection

Topic	Question
Vivid memories	What are your most vivid memories of those early years?
Being Hurt	Tell me about a time you were deeply hurt by your child.
Multiple Children	If you had more than one child how did you see their relationship with each other grow and develop through the years?
Resemblances	When you think of your children growing up who did they each resemble in personality and looks and why?
My Partner	What have you observed in your partner since you became parents?
Hopes and Dreams	What were your hopes and dreams for your children?
Keepsakes	What of your child's things have you kept from the time they were babies until today
Enriched My Life	Do you think having children has enriched your life?
Wisdom	What would you like to say to your children now?
Old Age	Do you expect your child to care for you and your partner in your old age?

Loss of a Child

Topic	Question
Coping	If you have been lost a child, how did you cope?
Ceremony	Was there a ceremony to mark his/her passing?
Feelings	In the weeks following your loss how did you feel?
Reflection	What would you change about your choices at the time?
Source of Strength	Who was your greatest source of strength following the death?
Pushing the Boundaries	Were there things you had to do but didn't feel able or ready for?
Sadness	Describe your grief in the time since your loss.
Memories	What things did you keep?

Grandchildren

Topic	Question
Meet the Grandchildren	When were your grandchildren born?
Where Are They Now	What age are they today and where do they live?

What It Is Like	What type of grandparent did you think you would be?
My Child is a Parent	How would you describe your son/daughter as a parent?
Quality of Life	How do your grandchildren live?
In a Perfect World	Ideally what kind of relationship would you like to have with each of your grandchildren?
Life Lessons	What lessons have you learned as a grandparent?
Family Stories	What stories do you tell your grandchildren about family members passed away?
Personalities	Tell me something about each grandchild that gives us a sense of who they are.
Lasting Impression	What lasting impression would you like to leave your grandchildren of you and your life?

Great Grandchildren

Topic	Question
Meet the Great Grandchildren	When were your great grandchildren born
Where Are They Now	What age are they today and where do they live?

What It Is Like	How did you imagine yourself as a great grandparent?
My Grandchild is a Parent	How would you describe your grandchild as a parent?
Quality of Life	How do your great grandchildren live?
In a Perfect World	Ideally what kind of relationship would you like to have with each of your great grandchildren?
Personalities	Tell me something about each great grandchild that gives us a sense of who they are.

Making the Time

"I don't have the time" is the most common reason people tell us they aren't progressing as quickly as they would like. Writing your life story takes time, motivation and inspiration.

No-one can expect to have the job finished in a day, and fitting it into our busy schedules can be difficult.

One of the best ways to stay on track is to allocate time on a regular basis. Each week you could pick a topic and write a few sentences, a few paragraphs or even a few pages. It doesn't matter how much you write, as long as you write something every week. It could take as little as 15 minutes.

If you do this for 52 weeks, you will have created a large part of your life story to share with your family and future generations at the end of just one year.

Of course you could use technology to help keep you on track. Try creating a recurring appointment in the calendar of your mobile phone and make sure you don't mark the appointment as complete until you have written about the topic you have selected. If you are busy, it doesn't matter if it stays on your screen as a gentle reminder for a day or two.

You could also signup for a free trial of StoriesKept by visiting www.storieskept.com

When you register for a free trial, you can optionally receive a memory prompt at the end of each week. We call this the "Storieskept Challenge" and it is designed to motivate you to get the job done.

A little bit about StoriesKept

> ***"I know I want to write my life story, but I'm not sure what to write about or how to make the time..."***

Sound familiar?

When we talk to people about writing their life story, this is the most common problem we hear. More often than not people download a list of questions with the best of intentions, but they never find the time, or find it difficult to stay organized when they are writing.

We also hear other common concerns...

... why do I have to write in historical order?

... how can I manage the photos and images in my story?

... how can I keep everything organized and in sequence?

... why is my word processor so slow and cumbersome?

... how do I format my story when I want to get it professionally printed?

... will I ever get it done?

Writing your life story doesn't just happen overnight. Recalling memories, organizing your writing and collating your photos takes time and commitment.

The point about memories is that they don't necessarily appear in chronological order! Writing in a word processor makes it incredibly difficult to keep things in the correct order.

If you have ever written a family history with a Word processor, you quickly come to terms with how things slow down as the size of the document increases. It doesn't take many images to make most word processors sluggish and almost grind to a halt.

Making sure the images are the right size, and that the page breaks are in the right places is another frustration. If you have ever gone back and edited an earlier piece of work, you will certainly understand how annoying it can when a small change can cause entire document to need reformatting.

When I was writing my family history I discovered first-hand how difficult it can be to prepare and format the final result for publishing. After looking at all the available solutions, I realized that there aren't actually solutions online that made it easy to do, and that maybe I should use my software skills to create a comprehensive and professional autobiography or memoir writing solution.

StoriesKept has been created from this need.

By curating an extensive list of deep and meaningful questions, and by including extensive publishing options and an online application, I believe that we have created a solution that will ensure your memories and dreams are treasured for many years to come.

I believe that we have created a simple system where family members can record their amazing stories at their own pace, and on their own terms. A solution that allows you to ignore questions that don't appeal to you, with the ability to upload images, edit previous memories and work in my own order. We have paid special attention to "magically" resizing photos and formatting to produce a perfect layout every time.

When it comes time to produce the final document, we allow you to export in a range of industry standard printing formats. Your entire life story will be instantly reformatted to match new book format and the requirements of a print-on-demand service to result in a lavishly illustrated story of your life.

Detailed Questions

Nearly every question included in this book has been presented as a single sentence memory prompt. This makes it very easy to look through the list and find a topic to write about and it will certainly give you a good checklist for your writing.

However, our online software includes a much more comprehensive version of each question. For example, the question about friendships is shown in this book as:

> "Tell me about friendships you had as a young child and when you were at primary school"

The online version of the question is

> "Tell me about friendships you had as a young child and when you were at primary school. Did you make friends easily? Who was your best friend and general playmates? How did you meet and what do you remember doing together? Have any of these friendships lasted? What fun did you have and what trouble did you get into together? How far away did you live from your friends? Where did you play? Did you stay at each other's house? How did you get there? Did you have anyone you didn't get on with? How did you deal with that?"

As you can see, the online version is significantly enhanced and can greatly enhance your life story by helping you to recall extra details about each topic.

If you are serious about writing your autobiography or memoir, it is well worth signing up for a free trial of StoriesKept. (at www.storieskept.com)

19656558R00046

Printed in Poland
by Amazon Fulfillment
Poland Sp. z o.o., Wrocław